W.O.

MW01031604

GET MUSCLE, STRENGTH AND STAMINA IN 30 MINUTES OR LESS

(Living the Fitness Series)

By Marc Holden

www.livingthefitness.com

amazon.com/author/marcholden

Living the fitness

ISBN-13: 978-1492941880

ISBN-10: 1492941883

Disclaimer

Not all exercise programs are suitable for everyone. Always consult your doctor before beginning any exercise program. I will not be responsible or liable for any injury sustained as a result of any fitness program presented in this book. The views expressed in this book are my opinions. Perform these exercises at your own risk.

TABLE OF CONTENTS

INTRODUCTION

Fitness takes commitment. If you are looking for an easy way to get fit, you will be looking for a long while. No matter what fitness program you encounter or try, you will see that all of them will yield some results with persistence and effort. Other than the military, the majority of fitness programs focused on only one aspect of health. In the 1980s there was the aerobics craze which definitely helped stamina, endurance, and cardiovascular health. Yet it did little for strength or core. Later, it was step aerobics, which tried to address the elements of strength and integrated the most important fitness move, the squat. After this there was Tae Bo, the Bow Flex, Spinning, Pilates and more. All of these have good components, but are not a complete fitness solution. In order to flesh out these programs, you had to add a serious round of nautilus machines and/or calisthenics. Unless you had a personal trainer, you probably did not participate in a complete fitness program.

You are reading this book because you are already pretty serious about getting fit. You have probably heard of CrossFit and know that it is intense and thorough. It is not for those who are not willing to stick with something. It is not a fad, not a trend, and not a gimmick. It is complete and total fitness. Whether you are already fairly fit and are looking for a challenge, or if you have been unfit your whole life and want to make change, CrossFit is for you. It is for all of you. Young, old, underweight or overweight, CrossFit will take you to your fitness nirvana. It works because it is based on sound principles and does not try to take short cuts.

As you read this book you will learn most of what there is learn about CrossFit. You may even go to the official CrossFit website and look at some of the hundreds of videos on their site. With each fact you learn you need to say your personal mantra of CrossFit is for people like me, "I can do this". At times you may feel intimidated, or feel that this program is only for "professionals". But these are false claims. CrossFit is for you. You are CrossFit. You can and will become amazingly fit with this program. CrossFit has been "discovered". It is not made up. It does not have a cute tag line like "Just Do It". It is bare bones in many ways. It takes the facts we know about fitness, our bodies and how our muscles work and combines these facts into a physical regimen that will always work. It cannot fail because it is revealed to us by the workings of our own bodies. With that said, CrossFit is not a cult. It is based on science. It uses technology when needed. You can and will be fit. Remember, you are a CrossFit athlete.

PART 1 - WHAT IS CROSSFIT?

FOUNDERS GREG AND LAUREN GLASSMAN

Physical fitness programs are ones that can be flash in the pans, or ones whose basic tenets are so well founded that they tend to last. Greg Glassman is one of those business entrepreneurs and fitness buffs who saw a need for a better fitness program that was flexible and applicable to many people's fitness needs. He noticed very early on that most people's fitness was unbalanced. This led to poor performance, shorter lives, and task specific skills that are not always useful for overall living.

A California native, Greg Glassman was always involved in fitness. As a college student, he worked in Pasadena, CA at the local YMCA as a trainer and later trained many celebrities between the years of 1974 or so and 1985. As Greg worked with different people with different abilities, all of whom had different goals, he began to realize the need for an all-inclusive fitness program. It during these years that he developed the key, broad stoke ideas for what would later become CrossFit.

In 1995 Glassman opened his first CrossFit gym not long after joining the Santa Cruz, CA police department. Once again, Glassman noticed that the men and women he was working with were not truly fit at all levels. Some had strength, some had stamina, a few had both, but overall Glassman felt that all his fellow officers had gaps in their fitness levels. Officers who were not fit were easier to kill. As CrossFit began to catch on, and workouts and videos were made to support the program, Glassman clearly identified the elements he felt were critical to a true fitness program. According to Barba, (2005), "The CrossFit program attempts to improve the 10 physical skills most commonly associated with physical fitness: cardio respiratory endurance, strength, flexibility, power, speed, coordination, accuracy, agility, balance and stamina" (1). What is somewhat unique in Glassman's approach is that there are no machines to use, nothing to buy. It is sometime describes as a "bare bones" workout. Anyone can do this fitness program, virtually anywhere (2). Glassman is not without his critics, and some go so far to argue that the CrossFit program is not healthy. But on the whole, CrossFit is accepted and is growing worldwide with over 4000 affiliates worldwide.

[1]   Barba, "CrossFit PHYSICAL TRAINING," *Law & Order*, June 2005, http://www.questia.com/read/1P3-862693271.

[2] Ashley Prest, "Powered by Passion," *Winnipeg Free Press*, June 8, 2013, http://www.questia.com/read/1P3-2990603611.

PRIMARY PURPOSE OF CROSSFIT

CrossFit was designed with one purpose: complete fitness. People who exercise regularly tend to focus on skills for dedicated tasks. For example, athletes need balance and speed, or runners need endurance, or average people want to burn calories. This regimen goes against the entire purpose of CrossFit (3). CrossFit runs on the premise that all skills are interrelated and all skills need to be mastered. This is completed by doing core and conditioning exercises.

The idea is to train people so that they can meet and master any task that comes their way; whether it is a tennis player who has to play an 11 hour match, or a stay at home mom who has to walk 5 miles with three kids because her car broke down, a CrossFit trained person can meet the demand. The way CrossFit is designed, participants engage in various high intensity tasks of movement. As Greg Glassman states "No aspect of functional movement is more important than their capacity to move large loads over long distances and to do so quickly" (4).

When you walk into a CrossFit gym, the first thing you will notice is that there are no nautilus machines. But you will see free weights, steps, ropes, huge barbells, sacks of sand and other non-traditional workout equipment. The exercises that are done in the gyms are different every day. CrossFit training yields its best results when done in a community with others who will push you and not let you stop or quit.

---

[3] http://journal.crossfit.com/2007/04/understanding-crossfit-by-greg.tpl

[4] http://journal.crossfit.com/2007/04/understanding-crossfit-by-greg.tpl

CrossFit is designed to be excruciating. For those who do not have experience lifting heavy weights or doing 100's of pull ups you will want to start very simply. The keystone exercise of CrossFit is the Workout of the Day or WOD. If you participate in a CrossFit Gym, this will be led by a certified trainer. For example, suppose the WOD is 100 pull ups (yes 100!). Not only will you do these, but you have to do them in a way that takes the most strength. In the case of pull ups, you will not be allowed to swing too much with your knees and then use that momentum to pull yourself over the bar, but never fear, the certified trainer will work with you so that you gain the basic strength in your core so you can ultimately do these. There is no shame or blame. One starts where they are.

An example of a conditioning exercise may be jump rope. If you think you know how to jump rope the CrossFit way, you may have to think again. You will not be allowed to jump back and forth and "cheat". You will have to jump exactly straight up and down, not too high, with smooth transitions. And you may have to do this 500 times.

CrossFit is an exercise regimen that focuses on core strength and conditioning. Without using machines, CrossFit is a sport of fitness that is best experienced in a community of other fitness athletes.

GLOBAL SPREAD OF CROSSFIT

CrossFit opened its first gym in 1995 and since then has grown to become an international sport; the sport of CrossFit. Most people who participate in CrossFit enjoy the competition, but this is not essential. To date there are over 4000 CrossFit affiliated gyms globally. But this does not count the likely thousands of gyms that do CrossFit activities but are not an official affiliate. One of the reasons for CrossFit's success and popularity is that it has become the training of choice for many police departments, just like it did for Greg Glassman's police force in Santa Cruz. CA. It has also become standard teaching for PE in many high schools across the United States, as well as many government agencies in North America.

Since CrossFit relies heavily on the idea of community, this has helped it grow globally. The Internet has made it possible for people to track their progress in online forums and blogs and to be told about upcoming events and competitions. The famed WOD (Workout of the Day) is broadcast online to gyms and personal computers everywhere. CrossFit now sponsors dozens of competitions and events worldwide. This too has helped to make CrossFit a household name in the world of fitness.

The CrossFit Games is a popular series of events that moves its location often to venues all over the world. It can also be accessed online. Here, hard core CrossFit athletes compete against each other. But besides this, anyone can compete in the CrossFit Games preliminary event even if they cannot get to the actual venue. The CrossFit Company posts the competition online under the heading "CrossFit Games" on its website. For those who want to see how they fair against CrossFit athletes, they can perform the exercises and then post their results online. From this pool of competitors, the top ranked athletes are invited to compete in a regional competition. And from here, winners are asked to compete in the actual CrossFit Games. In this way, the best of the best are selected from a global pool of competitors, making points and rankings earned even more meaningful. You can really see how you compare to others.

CrossFit Kids has also helped CrossFit become an international phenomenon. This program began in 2004 and is in 1200 gyms in North America, Australia, Africa, Europe, Japan and India. There are over 2000 CrossFit Kids trainers that teach CrossFit skills to kids and teens. Because CrossFit Kids is NOT scaled down in intensity, this has made the program have an excellent reputation and has increased its popularity. CrossFit Kids runs many school programs, both before and after school, as well as being the primary curriculum for many schools around the globe.

Because CrossFit is targeted at everyone, has super high expectations, and is an all-inclusive fitness program, it has taken off in popularity like wild fire. Everyone wants to be fit, even if they do not think they can. CrossFit not only appeals to this desire, it teaches that you CAN be fit. It is not a pipe dream. It is possible. With this positive message, and the quality program it is, it is no wonder that CrossFit is everywhere.

CROSSFIT TRAINING

CrossFit targets ten domains of fitness. These domains include cardiovascular and respiratory endurance, stamina, strength, flexibility, power, speed, coordination, balance, agility and accuracy. The entire philosophy of CrossFit training is that all ten of these areas must be trained in order to achieve true fitness. CrossFit is purposefully designed to be intense, physically demanding, and enervating. Because of this, it is optimal training for the military and athletes. But if you are not part of these groups, never fear. CrossFit is highly adaptable and can be adjusted to work with anybody and any skill level. Generally, it is recommended that you work with an affiliated gym for with a certified trainer, especially if you are a beginner fitness athlete. So, what does CrossFit training look like?

LIFTING WEIGHTS

CrossFit uses weights. And if you are looking at the CrossFit website for WOD or other games, you may notice that the prescribed weight is much more than you can lift. CrossFit targets CrossFit men, generally. But you can adapt the weight to meet your needs. You can use lighter barbells or even just a PVC pipe if you have to. Especially in the beginning stages, CrossFit training is very concerned with form; that is, how you lift a weight. CrossFit will ask that you maintain certain positions while lifting weights, and not try to work around form just to lift a weight (badly) once or twice. CrossFit's entire goal is to get you fit enough to lift weights with good form and range of motion. More important is the number of repetitions that you can complete using the correct form. So if the WOD asks for lifting 50 pounds over your head 25 times, then adjust as needed. But keep the 25 reps. Maybe lift 10 pounds 25 times with excellent form.

RESISTANCE TRAINING

CrossFit loves to use your own body weight as resistance for things like pull ups, squats, pushups and handstand pushups. For most people, these training exercises will have to be adapted. So, if you cannot do a handstand push up, then you can, instead, do pushups on an inclined plane by putting your feet on a box that is one foot off the ground. Again, what is important is form. So be sure to do form-perfect exercises, even if you cannot do the prescribed level of resistance.

To look at another example, suppose the WOD asks you to do squat while resting 250 LBS on your back shoulders. CrossFit considers the squat a basic movement and is prevalent in many training routines. Ok. For most of us, this is not possible today. So, instead, focus on doing the toughest squat you can. This may mean that you squat with no weights and a bar for support, but do 50. Or it may mean that you squat with 20 pounds across your shoulders, with no bar for support 5 times. Focus on form and range of motion and balance. These are the key elements to the CrossFit philosophy.

ENDURANCE

CrossFit never said that their routines were comfortable. You will be pushed to your limit and endurance training is one of the ways CrossFit does this. High intensity for CrossFit means high average. So, if a beginner fitness athlete can maintain 3.2 MPH on a treadmill for 30 minutes, a high averaged one would be able to maintain about a 4.2 MPH pace just to give you an idea. So, CrossFit wants you to push yourself to your limits, but not so much that you get sick or injure yourself. What is more important is that you are able to maintain the given activity for the length of time set (usually 20 minutes). You should be able to breathe even though you are pushing yourself to maintain a constant flow of motion.

Remember that for CrossFit, this is a sport: "the sport of fitness". So, like any sport, it is necessary to keep track of what you were able to accomplish during a training workout. CrossFit has two ways to measure progress; time and number of repetitions. There are many ways to record your progress. You can use "old school" ways like a journal or index cards. Or you can use iPhone apps and other online tools to record your WODs. Whatever method you use, be sure that you state any weight you used, or modification, and how long you were able to maintain the activity. So, if you did 30 squats, but needed the support of a bar, be sure to document this. One day, you will do 30 squats without any support. You will want to know how long it took you to be able to do this task.

PART 2 - CROSSFIT EXERCISES

You know you are losing the battle to get fit when the bench for your bench press has more empty longnecks around it than it does 25 pound plates. I am willing to bet that you don't even step on the scale anymore. This is either out of fear of what you will see, or the effort to step up onto something is too much for you. Here is a useful fact: the first step to getting back into shape is stepping onto the bathroom scale. This is because when the numbers stop spinning and you see what you weigh, your head is going to start spinning. Getting fat is gradual, and most people refuse to admit that they are gaining weight until they see the numbers on the scale. Studies have shown that people who step on a bathroom scale each morning are more prone to lose weight than those who don't. So, while you're thinking about it, go ahead and take that first step towards getting fit. Step onto your bathroom scale.

First off, even if you are not all that fat, the fact that you do not work out is slowing down your life.

Without exercise, people become sluggish. This leads to poor performances in all aspects of life. From keeping up with your children, to keeping up with the young bucks at work who are getting the promotions. It can even lead to a sluggish sex life. You probably think your level of fitness is just fine. Maybe it is. Maybe you are content with your level of fitness. That is the problem most people face every day, and they don't even know it. They are content with that which is not good enough. Perhaps you are fit. You are fit enough. However, fit enough for what? You probably are not fit enough to be cross fit.

Getting fit is the key to confidence. Confidence is the key to a successful life. Perhaps you are successful, despite not being as fit as you can be. I can see the grin spread across your face as you think the need to get into top shape doesn't apply to you. If you believe this, you are wrong, and that is because complacency begins in the mind, works its way into your body, and spreads out into your personal life.

People who are fat do not look like they have the qualities that most people admire. People admire those who are passionate, motivated, committed, and disciplined. Committing to a workout program requires all four of those characteristics. This means that when you stick to a workout program, not only are you getting in shape, but those four enviable characteristics are going to become a part of you, and they are going to begin to materializing in all facets of your everyday life. In other words, the simple act of working out is a life-changing habit.

Starting is hard. Perhaps it is even harder to start than it is to run that one extra lap, or push the barbell up over your shoulders for that one extra repetition.

BODYWEIGHT EXERCISES

AIR SQUAT

Stand erect, hands on hips. Keep your chest out and chin slightly up. Breathe in, keep your back straight, and stoop down. In the down position, your rear should be out and your thighs level. Breathe out as you go down, then breathe back in as you come up. These sets should be done as quickly as can be done while maintaining proper position. You will feel the results primarily in your gluteus and thighs, but this exercise works almost every muscle in your lower body.

BACK EXTENSION

Lie face down and cross your arms in front of you, palms down and overlapping. Rest your chin upon your palms. If you are more comfortable resting your head, face down upon your palms, do that. Breathe in, and then lift your head up at the same time you lift up your legs, breathing out as you do. You should try to raise your belly button off the floor. Your hands will remain on the ground. Hold this position for several seconds, and then return to the starting position. This exercise targets the lower back, and is sometimes beneficial if you are experiencing back pain.

BOX JUMP

This is an intense workout that is used to build explosive power in the legs. Rest longer in between reps than you normally do for other exercises. Be sure you are jumping onto a stationary box, and that the height is such that you can easily navigate it. Stand in a relaxed, athletic position in front of the box, and then quickly extend your arms back while going into a quarter squat. Immediately push off from that position to land on the box. Do not try to land heavy. Try to land light upon your feet. From on top of the box, repeat the process to jump back down from it. The primary muscles that benefit from this workout are the glutes, quads, hamstrings, and calves. The secondary muscles that enjoy this workout are the hip flexors. The hip flexors are the group of muscles that make the flexing of the hip joint possible.

BURPEE

Stand upright, hands upon hips. Quickly bend over in a squatting down position with your palms on the ground, and your arms straight. From this position, kick your legs out so that you come to rest in the pushup position. Your arms should be supporting your weight. Now, instead of kicking your legs out from under your position, kick them back underneath you, so that you have returned to the squatting position. Your hands should still be on the ground. From this position, jump up to the original hands on hips position. This exercise will burn about 50% more fat than regular weight training. It works the abs, hamstrings, front deltoids, the chest, and the arms. If you are only going to do one exercise, you should consider making this that exercise.

HANDSTAND PUSHUP

This exercise is easier said, than done. It is possible you will need a partner to hold your legs up. This is because just performing a handstand requires a great deal of strength and agility. If you have never performed a handstand, you will need a partner to spot you; otherwise you may break your neck. If you do not have a partner, but can do a handstand, do so near a wall so that the front of your legs can balance against it.

If you are using a partner, get in the pushup position with your arms extended. Your partner will then lift your legs until they are directly over you and you are upside down, arms extended in a handstand position. Now, perform as many handstand pushups as you can. Even one is a good start. This workout strengthens the triceps, the anterior and lateral deltoids, as well as the wrists and forearms. It also forces the body to use many muscles it ordinarily doesn't use, because it is struggling to balance itself.

JUMP ROPE

This exercise will burn about 10 calories per minute if you just do it at a moderate tempo. Crank it up a notch and you will burn 20 or more calories per minute. Use a couple of challenging tricks to keep things fresh. First, see if you can swing the rope beneath your feet twice with each jump. The most common trick seen is probably the criss-cross, which is actually pretty easy to master. At the top of the action, simply cross your arms. As soon as you jump through the loop this created, uncross them, and then cross again at the top.

KNEES-TO-ELBOWS

This is simple. Hang from a pull up bar and then bring your knees up until they touch your elbows. This is going to work your core to its foundation. Make sure to give your abs and your lats a good squeeze on the way up, so you can feel their contraction. This is also going to increase your grip strength. It is important to keep the move controlled on the way up, as well as on the way down. You should do as many as you can to failure. Of course, if you can not bring your knees up to your elbows, bring them as far up as you can in the beginning. From there, continuing to practice this move will eventually see your knees touching your elbows.

L-SIT

This is the basic, must-have move for all acrobats. It requires tremendous abdominal strength to perform. This exercise will strengthen all your core muscles, and your quads and lats as well. There are various ways to perform this move. Ideally, you will have parallel bars. However, dip bars or even push up bars or chairs will work also. You can even do them straight off the floor. This is the hardest, however, because of the slight clearance.

To start an L-sit, let's assume you are using push up bars on a floor. To start, sit in between bars and grasp them with your knuckles facing out. Next, push down so that your rear rises off the floor. Do not shrug. Make a strong push down. Your rear should be right below your shoulders. If you are advanced, you can now spread your legs out directly in front of you so that your body forms an L. Stay like that for several seconds, lower, and start again. If that is too hard, just make it so your toes touch the ground, and try to lift one leg at a time. That is a good starting point until you can eventually lift the other leg, and finally, spread them out in front to form the L.

LUNGE

This is great for the thighs; pure and simple. Put your hands just out from your sides. If you like, you may grasp 2-5 pound dumbbells in them. Keep your back straight, and look ahead, not down. Take a step with your right foot and hold. It should look like you're about to strike out in that direction. Now bend your right leg down until your thigh is level with the floor. Your left leg will bend as well, and that's fine. Hold it a second and return to the beginning position. Now, do the same thing, but start with your left foot.

PULL UP

This is the standard exercise you first learned back in Junior high or sooner. In order for it to be effective, you need to begin from a hanging position on the bar, with the forward grip. This means your knuckles are facing you. From that dangling start, pull yourself up until your chin is over the bar. The legs must remain motionless. Some people will cross their ankles to help keep their legs from moving. This classic exercise builds the forearms and triceps, as well as the upper back muscles. To really ad width to your lats and get that wide-shouldered look, place your hands about six inches wider on each side of the bar.

Muscle Up

This is a move that takes the pull up to a whole new dimension. To do this, simply perform the first part of the pull up. That is, pull up until your chin is over the bar. Then, instead of going back down, muscle up on this move. Do this by pushing down on the bar until you have raised yourself all the way up, which means the bar will be just below your belt, instead of at your chin. However, to achieve this, it should be completed as one entire move, from pull up to the muscle up. You will need to explode your knees upward as you go to help with momentum. As you begin your push for the muscle up part, lean in on the bar when it is at your belly. This is an amazing move for bulking up the triceps.

Pushup

It's amazing how many people still get the standard pushup wrong. The body must be straight as a plank. Hands shoulder width apart, palms flat, and the toes, pointing down, supporting the other end of the body. The head should look down. Start in the up position, and take a deep breath. Lower yourself to your chest as you breathe out. Raise yourself back up as you breathe in. Many people are tempted to touch their stomach to the floor on the downward movement. That is incorrect. The chest must touch. The pecs, deltoids and triceps are the major muscles that benefit from the pushup.

Ring Dip

The ring dip is one of the most challenging workouts for the triceps, while also affecting the shoulders and chest. Many other muscles are called into play to help stabilize the body because of the motion of the rings. As with a bar dip, grasp the rings knuckles out. The elbows must be tucked close to the sides, and pointing straight back. Tuck the legs at a 45-degree angle and push down until your arms are fully extended. Lower yourself until your hands are about level with your armpits, and then raise yourself again. It is imperative that the legs do not swing or kick.

Rope Climb

There is an art to climbing rope, and there are many methods that do not work. Many people remember being taught that they should use the sides of their feet to grab the rope and push up with in concert with the arms. Too often, the feet slip, and leave the rope climber flailing around without going anywhere. The following method should yield satisfactory results.

Address the rope with it hanging down the middle of your legs. Raise your right or dominant hand all the way up, and grasp the rope as though you are holding a torch. Next, you are going to lift your right leg up, knee bent, like a marching move. Wrap that leg around the rope so that the inside of your knee is hooking the rope. Continue around so the rope wraps around your Achilles, and then extend your leg. The lower end of the rope should be draped around the top of your shoe.

Now, meet your right hand up the rope with your left hand, and swing your left leg over your right leg, with the left ankle locking over the right ankle. You are now in a secure holding pattern on the rope. To move up the rope, release your left leg, keeping the rope wrapped the way it is around the right leg. Move your rear end up, pull up with your hands, and then lock the left ankle back over the rope on the right ankle. You are now in a comfortable holding pattern again, but have moved up the rope one notch. After some practice, you will be able to scale ropes without the effort displayed by many people who do not know this method. Rope climbing is an integral part of training for armed forces around the world because it works so many muscles. The Besides strengthening the fingers and hands, most of the muscles in the forearm are affected, as well as the shoulders, triceps, and leg muscles.

Sᴉᴛ Uᴘ

The classic sit up is done with the legs bent at a 30-degree angle, feet flat on the floor, and the hands behind the head. The hands may not be used to help leverage the maneuver, however, because it can lead to injury, and the muscles will not receive the benefit of the workout. If you cannot perform this exercise without pulling on your neck with your hands, cross your hands in front of your chest.

Breathe out as you lift up, touching elbows to knees, and breathe out on the way down. The sit up works the hip flexors and abdominal muscles under the sternum and above the pelvis. This move should be done in a slow and methodical manner. The average needed for a good workout is about 30 reps, after that, your form will tend to become sloppy, and this can lead to injury. The abdominal muscles are able to recover each day, so you can use this workout on a daily basis if you like. If any part of your body feels sore after a workout other than the abdominal muscles, seek professional help before continuing this particular workout.

TOES-TO-BAR

Toes-to-bar is another great movement for the core muscles that help keep the center of your body stabilized. It also helps develop strong forearms, fingers, abs, hip flexors, pecs, and lats. For this exercise, you will need your pull up bar again. With a shoulder wide grip, and your knuckles facing you, hang from the bar. Now, in a slow, fluid movement, bring your legs up straight until your toes touch the bar. Bring them back down in the same controlled manner. Do as many of these as you can to failure. If you cannot touch the bar, come as close as you can.

Mono Structural Movements

Running

Many people do not stretch before they run. It is considered more important to give the muscles a slight warm-up first. If you do stretch, be sure to include the calves, hamstrings, and thighs. There is a proper form for running. The strides should be light and medium, landing lightly on the center of your feet each time. If you run on the balls of your feet, your shins are going to become painful. If you are landing on your heels, you are over-striding.

Do not take high, bouncing steps. This will begin to jar your body and bones, and wear you out before you can go very far. There is no need to lift your feet that high off the ground. Use easy, low strides, landing on the center of the foot. Your eyes should be focused on the ground about 15 feet ahead. Don't clench your fists, leave them lightly folded, holding air. Keep your posture erect, and don't slump your shoulders, because this will interfere with your breathing.

Practice breathing from your belly, and not your chest. Shallow chest breathing will give you less air and cause the painful side aches people get when running. Elbows should be bent 90-degrees, and your hands should swing from the shoulder. The elbows should be kept close to your side, and your hands should swing forward to back, not side-to-side, with the hands almost meeting in the center. Besides toning muscle and giving the heart a good workout, an average one mile run at about 6 mph can burn up to 1,000 calories for an average sized person.

ROWING

Rowing is a high-intensity workout. It is both a calorie burner and a major strength builder. However, one of the most common injuries suffered by rowers is the lower back. This is sometimes due to improper form or over-doing it. Anybody who begins rowing and feels discomfort in the lower back should stop immediately and get a professional opinion before continuing.

There is a lot of confusion on the part of people who either are just starting to row. They have varied ideas on how to do it, and therefore, many do it incorrectly. Rowing, however, is simple. You are using your legs first, then your core, and finishing with your arms. This is not a herky-jerky motion. After gripping the handle, or handles, you first push back with your legs. After they reach their full extension, lean back with your core. Finish the movement by pulling back with your arms.

The return movement will be the opposite of what you have just done. Go forward with the arms, lean in with your core, or the abdominals and their surrounding muscles, and then go in with the legs. Once you have those three movements down, you may begin to work on building up speed for high-volume reps. In addition to burning an amazing amount of calories and building strength in your quads, lats, and core, your biceps and triceps are also getting a dual workout.

Movements with Weights

Dead Lift

This underrated move should be a part of your staple of weightlifting. It is called the dead lift, because you are lifting dead weight. There is no momentum to help you. This is one of the best weight lifting moves, and one of the most primal. Approach the barbell, which will just be sitting on the ground. Your feet need to be shoulder width, and your grip should be just wider than your feet. Your grip will be knuckles facing you. On heavier lifts, some people use one set of knuckles facing them, and the other set facing down.

Your stance is important. While this is a simple lift, it is beneficial to almost every muscle you have, but if done wrong, it can deal damage. You must keep your back straight throughout the entire move, both up and down. Your head will face straight throughout the move, and not up or down. When you bend down to pick up the barbell, you must remember you are bending down; you are not bending over.

In fact, it is a good tip, when bending down, to imagine there is a hundred dollar bill on the ground in front of you that you need to pick up. However, a man is standing in front of you whom you don't trust. Bend down to address the bar with this in mind, but keep your eyes ahead, do not look up. You are now gripping the barbell, so stand back up. Remember, you are lifting with your legs, not your back. Keep the bar as close to your body as possible on your way up. You can almost make it kiss your shins, knees, and belt buckle. Now lower it in the exact same manner. Do not hurry. Pause at the top, and go back down in a deliberate manner. This move calls into play almost every muscle in your body without even lifting it over your head.

CLEAN

This begins like the dead lift, but continues to the point where you lift the barbell over your head. Approach the barbell in the same way as with the dead lift, and pull the weight up to your waist in the same deliberate motion as before. However, after you have the barbell at your waist, in an explosive manner bring it up to your chest and then lift it over your head. This movement increases your overall power, and particularly works the hamstrings, calves, gluteus, and upper and lower back.

KETTLEBELL SWING

Grip the kettlebell with your knuckles facing you. Your legs will be bent at about a 45-degree angle, and your back will be straight, although you will bend at the waist. Be sure your head faces straight, and that you don't let it droop or look down. This will lead to poor form which can hurt your lower back. Keep your glutes clenched, and swing the kettlebell between your legs in a backward motion, like you are hiking a football, and then bring it back up in front of you at arms length. This should be done in one continues motion, and you should not stop until you reach failure. Keep the ball close to your pelvic region on the under swing. Some people let it fall to far, and this may lead to lower back injury as well. This workout will mainly affect the lower back, quads, hips, thighs, hamstrings, and shoulders.

PRESS

The standard press should be done in this manner. Bring the barbell up to your waist in the dead lift form. From there, bring it up clavicle high, with your forearms pointing up, the bar resting in the palms of your hands, and your elbows in front of your forearms.

Keep your weight upon your heels, squeeze your glutes so that you don't arch your back, and then press the barbell up until your arms are fully extended. You should drive the weight upward with your heels pushing into the ground. Breath out on the way up, and in on the way down. These repetitions should be done in a deliberate manner so that the move is done properly, and the muscles enjoy the intended impact of the movements. The primary muscles this lift builds are the muscles in the core, the deltoids in the shoulders, and the triceps.

SNATCH

This is one of the most advanced moves anybody in the muscle building field can complete. The approach will have you bending over to grip the barbell. You will need a wide grip, almost all the way to the ends of the bar, while your feet will be shoulder width. Squat down to where your buttock is parallel to the ground. Your back should be straight. You must then simultaneously rise out of the squat while lifting the barbell behind your head with the arms fully extended. You then drop back into a squat.

While the barbell remains extended upward behind your head, and then lift out of the squat to a standing position with the barbell still over your head. From this position, some people just drop the weights if they have bumper plates. Others choose to lower the barbell as though in a reverse upright row, and then lower it to the ground.

SQUAT

This is another all around power exercise used by athletes. It is not generally done for cosmetic purposes. You should address the rack with the barbell placed about nipple high. Your grip will be just wider than shoulder width, knuckles facing you. Your feet will be shoulder width. Duck under the bar and let it rest on your posterior deltoids or right on the base of the neck on the flat part.

Tense up your upper back muscles in order to help stabilize your spine. Take a step back with your left foot, and another step back with your right. Make sure your feet are still shoulder width when you're done. You don't need to look up, but rather keep your head in a neutral position. Do this by watching the part of the room where the floor is met by the wall. To help keep your back in the right position, squeeze your chest muscles up.

Before you bend your legs, you must first thrust your hips back. With all of this accomplished, you may use your legs to begin your decent into a squatting position. Be sure to maintain your weight on the heels of your feet. Your knees should be aligned with your toes. It is important to lower yourself into a full squat. Many lifters do not go down far enough, and this will have adverse effects on them later, if they continue to do the exercise in this manner. To perform a full squat, your buttocks must be lower than the line your knees create. On the way back up, drive with the heels of your feet. At the top of the movement, lock your knees, wait a second, and then begin the next repetition.

SUMO DEADLIFT HIGH PULL

For this move, squat down to the bar with your feet shoulder-length apart, and your hands about six inches apart. Your thighs should be almost parallel to the ground. You should lean about 45-degrees forward, and keep your back straight. Your head should be at a slight upward angle. This exercise is done in one movement, and you will rise up from the squatted down position while pulling the barbell up under your chin as soon as your legs are straight. You will return to the starting position in one motion, and begin the next repetition. While regular dead lifts seem to emphasize the spinal erectors and the back, the sumo deadlift offers more benefits to the glutes, quads, hips, hamstrings, and upper traps.

THRUSTER

With this move, you will grip the barbell with a shoulder-wide grip, knuckles facing you, and feet spread shoulder-wide. You will clean the barbell up to your chest and bring it to rest across your shoulders. Your palms should face up. From here, you will go into a full squat. Your rear end should be just below your knees, with your elbows almost parallel to the ground, with your knees outside of the elbows. Your back will be straight, and you will be leaning forward at about a 45-degree angle, and your head will be straight, with your eyes looking ahead. From this position, you will explode upward. Your legs and hips must extend before you bring the bar up. As soon as your legs are straight and your hips extended, lift the bar over your head and lock your elbows. This is one repetition.

TIRE FLIP

This exercise is pretty much just what it sounds like. However, it is one of the more dangerous exercises there are, and it is recommended that a partner be nearby to help should something start to go wrong. A large tractor tire is used, and you can usually find one at a rental yard where they would love to lose some of their excess tires laying around. Tractor tires can weight anywhere from a couple hundred pounds to over 1200 pounds. That is 1200 pounds that will have a mind of its own if you lose control of it. The basic move is to lift it, push it forward and get a knee to it until it is upright. After that, it's a simple matter of pushing it back over. The secret to tire flipping is to move forward on a continuing basis without pausing. Keep moving forward on the tire.

This workout is used to increase explosive power and endurance in the individual. Many football coaches employ tire flipping, because the exercise mimics the move and raw power that football players need to come off the line of scrimmage in an explosive manner during games. The first move is to address the tire, which will be lying on its side, with your feet at a shoulder-wide stance. Next, squat down and bring your hands under the tire. Your hands should be a shoulder length apart, and your chest should now be touching the tire. If it isn't, move your hands out a little wider. You need to get your weight onto the front of your feet, so start moving them back until you can feel the shifting of the weight on your feet moving to the front of them.

Take a moment to picture yourself moving through the tire, and then make the beginning move by exploding forward with your legs. Your arms are not meant to lift this tire, so do not try to use them in a lifting manner, or you may hurt yourself. Your arms should be like two driving rods working in concert with your pumping legs, your hips, and your chest to drive the tire forward. As soon as the tire is as high as your waist, lift a knee and use it to help push the tire onto its tread. Right after you have thrust a knee into the tire, flip your hands around to palms out, and continue to drive with your legs, pushing with your arms. This will bring the tire onto its treads, and you can now push it over and start again.

It is important to know that any loss of momentum may result in a failure of the move. If at any time you feel the tire winning the battle, spin out of the way and let it fall. You can use lighter tires to do more reps and gain more stamina, or heavier tires for that short, explosive burst all athletes need.

WALL BALL

This should be what basketball players who can't hit their free throws are punished with. This move is basically a torturous version of shooting free throws. You will need a couple of medicine balls. The weight will depend upon what you can handle for one ball. The other needs to be large enough for you to spring off of with your buttocks.

Pretty much, you are going to throw a heavy wall up at a target on a wall, catch it, lower yourself enough to just bounce off the ball underneath you, and then repeat the process. However, as with all workouts, there is more than meets the eye. In simple terms, you could say it is a squat combined with a thrust.

A good lumbar curve of the back should be maintained for this workout, and the heels of the shoes should remain on the ground, though at the top of the move they may rise slightly off the ground. Start from a standing position a couple of feet away from a wall. It is important to have a target on the wall, or your throws will become lower and lower without your noticing. The target should be high enough that you can hit it comfortably a few times. The target need only be a mark of chalk. You are going to squat down, touch the ball behind you with your behind, drive up, or thrust, throw, catch, squat, and repeat. You should make this one motion, and throw until failure.

The ball should be kept close to your chin and chest at all times. You should be driving with your legs and releasing the ball as your legs straighten out. You want to keep your back straight and planing forward at an angle, rather than straight up and down, because at that point, you will become susceptible to injury. This exercise is excellent for the core muscles of the lower back and abdomen. It also improves endurance, as well as strengthens the legs, chest, and shoulders.

PART 3 – DIET AND NUTRITION

IMPORTANCE OF DIET IN A WEIGHT MANAGEMENT PROGRAM

There is no getting around the importance of diet in any weight management program. Many myths about eating have been debunked, such as skipping meals to reduce calories and hence lose weight (5). Successful programs, such as Weight Watchers, focus on portion control as the number one factor in diet and weight loss. In short the mantra is "you can eat anything you want, just not a lot of it".

With this said, it is also critical that you include variety in your diet. These are the Daily 5: Fruits, Vegetables, Grains, Proteins, and Oils.

The first step is to be aware of what you eat. Many of us mindlessly pop chips or crackers in our mouths like it is nothing. The fact is that the balance of fat, oils, grains and protein of "snacks" like this are often skewed to our disadvantage. To give you an example: Weight Watchers uses a point system based on the relationship of ingredients to nutritive value. If I am allowed 26 points in a day, eating one Nutri-Grain bar uses 4 of my points. Suppose later, I eat a bag of chips (another 8 points). That's a lot of points for not a lot of food. So, look around and see if you are guilty of things like this.

---

[5] http://www.choosemyplate.gov/food-groups/

Replace fruits and vegetable for those empty crackers and chips. It will be tough at first, because our bodies crave the salt and carbs we are used to feeding it. But, when it comes to fruits and vegetable, you can eat a lot.

A lot of what you consume everyday should be fruits and vegetables. So, when you feel hungry, eat an orange, nosh on carrots or soy beans. You can eat these things all day and there is only goodness for your health.

Next, the second most important key to your success in losing weight (or rather inches) is portion control. Let's say that again: portion control. Many people ignore the serving size notification on foods they buy. So if I buy a ham sandwich and read the label carefully, I may see that there are 3 servings. But if I alone eat the entire sandwich, I have eaten three times what is allotted me. You will be surprised how small a serving size is. Try measuring out ¼ cup of almonds, or 8 oz of juice. Then look at how much is sold in packages at the store. You will likely find that what you eat in one sitting is really 3 or 4 serving's worth. Restaurants are notorious for piling on 5 or 10 servings on a plate. Eat some, but leave most of it, or take it home.

CrossFit will certainly help you with your fitness and weight loss. But it will not do it without some serious changes about how you relate to food and how much you have been used to eating. As you gain lean muscle mass, you will be able to consume more. But until then, carry around a measuring cup set so you can be reminded about the portions you should be eating.

RECOMMENDED DIET FOR CROSSFIT

Serious CrossFit athletes adhere to a mathematical and strict dietary regimen. CrossFit focuses on protein, carbohydrates, fat and calories. In many ways the CrossFit diet is similar to many other recommended diets and healthy living habits. The bit difference may be the philosophy about calorie intake. CrossFit is a strong proponent in reducing calorie intake for a longer and healthier life. Here is a breakdown of the CrossFit diet.

The recommended diet is that protein be about 30% of your entire calorie intake per day. Protein is critical for cell growth and repair, and since Crossfit is very intense, CrossFit athletes need to pay close attention to the protein they eat. The key here is lean protein. Some examples of lean protein are fish such as tuna and salmon. Each is very high in protein and low in saturated fats. Saturated fats need to be avoided to maintain a healthy heart. Soy beans are another great source of protein. They are excellent because they contain all of the essential amino acids such as tryptophan and leucine. Of all 20 amino acids, 9 are essential and you can get them all with soybeans. As an added bonus, soybeans have fiber and Omega 3.

Carbohydrates are usually the things people love to eat, like pasta and breads. For the CrossFit diet, the carbohydrates you eat need to be low-glycemic. Glycemic refers to something called the glycemic index. This quantifies how quickly food is digested and turned into glucose and then enters the blood stream. High glycemic foods are usually the "bad" food that we love but should not eat like fruit juices, breads, potatoes, sweets and baked goods. All of the "bad" carbs lack fiber and protein which makes them release sugar too fast into your body. These need to be avoided. Low glycemic foods are ones like oatmeal, beans and vegetables. These are full of fat (the good kind), fiber and protein and cause a slow, steady digestion, making you feel full longer. The CrossFit diet recommends that about 40% of your daily calories should be from low glycemic carbohydrates. Cross Fit often refers to their diet as the "Caveman" diet (6). In other words, any food that has a "shelf life" or is processed in any way should be avoided. Processed foods tend to have high sugar counts, lower fiber and too much of bad fat and calories. As a general rule, you should eat what a caveman could eat. It should be fresh.

Fats are needed for our bodies to work properly. But these fats need to be monounsaturated and eaten in moderation. Replace monounsaturated fats for saturated or transfats. Monounsaturated fats can help reduce bad cholesterol levels in your blood and they provide nutrients to help develop and maintain your body's cells. Monounsaturated fats are also usually a good source of vitamin E, an antioxidant vitamin many people need more of in their diets. The CrossFit diet recommends that these fats be about 30% of your calories every day. Foods high in monounsaturated fats are olive and canola oils, avocados, nuts, seeds and peanut butter.

The recommended CrossFit diet is based on science and it easy to follow. There is nothing too difficult about it, especially if you have already isolated your poor eating habits and are working to eliminate them.

---

6 http://www.crossfit.com/cf-info/start-diet.html

Paleo and Zone Diets

In the last section we talked about the CrossFit Diet. There we touched a little bit about something called the Caveman diet, which simply put means to eat only fresh food, lean meats and lots of fruits and vegetables. Another name for this is the Paleo diet.

If you want to learn everything about the Paleo diet, check out my book *"Paleo for Athletes: Lose Weight and Get Muscle Quickly and Easily With The Paleo Solution"* at Amazon.com

The Paleo Diet is a way of living and eating that takes into consideration the fact that food evolution and processing has happened a lot faster than the human body has evolved. So, while food technology allows for astounding things to be done to make food edible longer, the human body is still, well, stuck in the Paleolithic era.

This means that genetically speaking, our bodies really cannot handle all the changes that happen to foods during all the modern "processing". As a result, we get acne, cancer, are fat, have heart problems, diabetes and all kinds of other health problems. According to some (7) the Paleo is the world's healthiest diet. In short, don't eat anything that was not available or cooked in a way our Paleolithic ancestors could have eaten.

Another diet that is endorsed by CrossFit is the Zone Diet (8). This is a diet that was developed by Barry Sears, M.D. and is a nutritional

[7] http://crossfitnewhaven.com/nutrition/

[8] http://journal.crossfit.com/2004/05/zone-meal-plans-crossfit-journ.tpl

regimen that allows you to attain your best physical performance. The Zone diet is based on the idea of "blocks". A block is a measurement of how much protein, carbs and fat is in food. By definition, a block equals 7 grams of protein, 9 grams of carbs, and 1.5 grams of fat. The goal is to equally represent these elements in every meal you eat. The Zone Diet sets out for you how many Blocks you should be eating at each meal. For example, if I am a small female, I should be eating, 10 blocks per day; 2 for breakfast, lunch and dinner plus two 2 block snacks. If I am a super stud, I would be a 5 block male who eats a total of 25 blocks per day.

What does a meal on the Zone diet look like? Well, here is an example from Greg Glassman himself (9). If I am that 2 block female, this is one possibility for what I may have for breakfast:

Breakfast Sandwich

1/2 pita bread

1 egg (scrambled or fried)

1 oz cheese

Served with 2 macadamia nuts

If I am a 5 block super stud, my breakfast could be this:

Breakfast Sandwich

1/2 pita bread

2 eggs (scrambled or fried)

2 oz cheese

---

[9] http://library.crossfit.com/free/pdf/cfjissue21_May04.pdf

1 oz ham, sliced

Serve with 1 1/2 apple

You may be thinking that is so detailed. Really "two macadamia nuts"? The answer is YES. This is how exacting one has to be if they are serious about their fitness. Think of star athletes like Novak Djokovic. His diet is so controlled he eats exact amounts of foods regularly and he has not had a piece of chocolate cake in over 10 years (or so the rumor goes). In any event, diet is a large part of his success and any pro athlete will say the same. So if you are a CrossFit athlete, you need to worry about and change your diet too.

PART 4 – PALEO RECIPES TO GET YOU STARTED (BONUS)

In this section you'll find 10 recipes of the Paleo diet to get you started with your Crossfit workouts. Most of these have a lot of protein, the building blocks of the body. Athletes, like you, need enough protein to repair and build muscle that is broken down during exercise. Enjoy!

If you like this diet, you can get an in depth description about the Paleo diet (including 50 recipes) in my book *'Paleo for Athletes: Lose Weight and Get Muscle Quickly and Easily with the Paleo Solution'* at Amazon.com.

CHICKEN & VEGGIE STEW

Cooking time: 50 minutes
Prep time: 10 minutes
Serves: 4

Ingredients:

3 tablespoons coconut oil
3 pounds chicken, cubed
1 large onion, chopped
¼ cup coconut flour
4 cups chicken broth
1 cup fresh peas, shelled
2 cups carrots, peeled and sliced
½ cup mushrooms, sliced
1 cup celery stalks, chopped
Salt and black pepper, to taste
1 cup coconut milk
2 tablespoons fresh cilantro, chopped

Instructions:

1. In a large pan, heat oil on medium-high heat.

2. Add chicken and cook till browned.

3. Transfer chicken to a plate.

4. Add onion and sauté for about 3 to 4 minutes.

5. Stir in coconut flour.

6. Add 2 cups broth and whisk lightly.

7. Boil for 1 minute.

8. Add remaining broth, peas, carrots, mushrooms and celery.

9. Season with salt and black pepper.

10. Reduce heat to medium-low.

11. Cover and simmer for 30 minutes.

12. Add coconut milk and cook for 10 minutes more.

13. Garnish with chopped cilantro and serve.

Nutritional Facts Per Serving:

Calories: 852
Fats: 24.9g
Carbohydrates: 17.9g
Proteins: 108.3g

FISH STEW

Cooking time: 15 minutes
Prep time: 15 minutes
Serves: 4

Ingredients:

2 tablespoons coconut oil

1 medium onion, chopped

5 cloves garlic, chopped

3 tomatoes, chopped

Salt and black pepper, to taste

2 tablespoons ground cumin

1 ½ cups coconut milk

2 pounds white fish fillets, cubed

2 tablespoons fresh cilantro, chopped

Instructions:

1. In a large pan, heat oil on medium-high heat.

2. Sauté onion for about 4 to 5 minutes.

3. Add garlic and sauté for 1 minute more.

4. Add tomatoes, salt, pepper and cumin and cook, stirring for 4 to 5 minutes.

5. Add coconut milk and bring to a simmer.

6. Add fish and cook for 4 to 5 minutes or until fish is done completely.

7. Garnish with cilantro.

Nutritional Facts Per Serving:

Calories: 700
Fats: 46.1g
Carbohydrates: 13.7g
Proteins: 59.4g

HERBED BEEF STEW

Cooking time: 50 minutes
Prep time: 10 minutes
Serves: 4

Ingredients:

2 tablespoons coconut oil
1 large onion, chopped
4 stalks celery, chopped
4 carrots, peeled and chopped
1 pound boneless beef, cubed
1 cup tomatoes, chopped
5 cups beef broth
½ teaspoon fresh thyme, chopped
½ teaspoon fresh rosemary, chopped
Salt and black peppers, to taste

Instructions:

1. In a pan, heat oil on medium-high heat.

2. Add, onion, celery and carrots and sauté for 4 to 5 minutes.

3. Add remaining ingredients and bring to a boil.

4. Reduce heat to medium-low.

5. Cover and simmer for, stirring occasionally for about 1 hour.

6. Uncover and cook for 40 to 45 minutes more.

Nutritional Facts Per Serving:

Calories: 372
Fats: 18.4g
Carbohydrates: 29.3g
Proteins: 25.9g

CHICKEN STIR FRY

Cooking time: 15 minutes
Prep time: 5 minutes
Serves: 4

Ingredients:

1½ cups coconut milk
1 teaspoon fresh ginger, grated
1½ teaspoon curry powder
Salt and black pepper, to taste
2 tablespoons coconut oil
1 pound boneless chicken breasts, cut into thin slices
1 small onion, chopped finely
1½ cups carrot, peeled and cut into thin slices
2 cups fresh spinach, trimmed and chopped

Instructions:

1. In a bowl, add coconut milk, ginger, curry powder, salt and black pepper and mix well.Keep aside.

2. In a skillet, heat oil on medium heat.

3. Stir fry chicken till golden.

4. Remove the chicken from skillet.

5. Add onion to the same pan and stir fry for about 2 minutes.

6. Add carrots and stir fry for about 4 minutes.

7. Now, add in chicken, coconut sauce and spinach.

8. Cook for 4 to 5 minutes or till spinach is just wilted.

Nutritional Facts Per Serving:

Calories: 513
Fats: 37.0g
Carbohydrates: 11.8g
Proteins: 36.0g

Grilled Fish with Advocado Salsa

Cooking time: 20 minutes
Prep time: 1 hour 10 minutes
Serves: 8

Ingredients:

For Grilled Fish

2 tablespoons coconut oil, melted
2 cloves garlic, minced
Pinch of cayenne pepper
1 teaspoons raw honey
2 lemons, juiced
Salt and black pepper, to taste
4 swordfish fillets

For Salsa

2 avocadoes, pitted and diced
3 peaches, pitted and diced
½ red onion, chopped
1 cloves garlic, minced
2 limes, juiced
Salt, to taste
1 tablespoon fresh cilantro, chopped

Instructions:

1. In a bowl, add oil, garlic, cayenne pepper, honey, lemon juice, salt and black pepper and mix well.

2. Add fish fillets and coat well.

3. Refrigerate for 1 hour to marinate.

4. Meanwhile in a bowl, mix all salsa ingredients. Refrigerate to chill.

5. Heat the grill to medium heat.

6. Grill fish fillets for 4 to5 minutes per side.

7. Place grilled fish in serving plate.

8. Top with salsa and serve.

Nutritional Facts Per Serving:

Calories: 394
Fats: 26.1g
Carbohydrates: 19.1g
Proteins: 24.6g

Citrus Roast Chicken

Cooking time: 1 hour 5 minutes
Prep time: 20 minutes
Serves: 4

Ingredients:

4 tablespoons coconut oil, melted
1 orange, zest grated and cut into quarters
1 lemon, zest grated and cut into quarters
3 tablespoons fresh ginger, grated and divided
1 (1½ pounds) whole chicken
Salt and black pepper, to taste
1 orange, juiced
2 lemons, juiced

Instructions:

1. Preheat the oven to 425 degrees F or 220 degrees C.

2. In a bowl, mix citrus zest, 1 tablespoon ginger, salt and black pepper. Keep aside.

3. With a sharp knife, make deep cuts in chicken.

4. Rub the citrus mixture in chicken cavities evenly.

5. Add the quartered orange and lemon inside the cavity.

6. In another bowl, add melted coconut oil, citrus juice and remaining ginger and mix well.

7. Brush the chicken with oil mixture evenly.

8. Place chicken in roasting pan.

9. Roast for 15 minutes.

10. Reduce heat to 375 degrees F (190 degrees C).

11. Brush chicken again and roast for 25 minutes.

12. After 25 minute, brush again and roast for further 25 minutes.

Nutritional Facts Per Serving:

Calories: 444
Fat: 19.2g
Carbohydrates: 17.8g
Protein: 51.0g

Roasted Sweet Potatoes, Chicken & Egg Salad

Cooking time: 25 minutes
Prep time: 20 minutes
Serves: 4

Ingredients:

For Salad

2 cups sweet potatoes, diced
2 tablespoons coconut oil, melted
2 cups cooked chicken, shredded
5 eggs, hard boiled and diced
1 white onion, chopped finely

For Dressing

1¼ cups avocado oil
1½ teaspoons Dijon mustard
½ teaspoon dried thyme
½ teaspoon dried parsley
½ teaspoon dried basil
2 teaspoon lemon juice
3 eggs
Salt and black pepper, to taste

Instructions:

1. Preheat the oven to 400 degrees F (200 degrees C).

2. Coat the sweet potato with oil evenly.

3. Spread sweet potato on baking sheet.

4. Roast for 20 to 25 minutes or till tender. Let it cool.

5. In a blender, add all dressing ingredients and blend till creamy and smooth.

6. In a serving bowl, add salad ingredients and dressing and mix well.

Nutritional Facts Per Serving:

Calories: 318
Fat: 24.6g
Carbohydrates: 28.2g
Protein: 33.8g

Beef Steak with Mushrooms & Asparagus

Cooking time: 15 minutes
Prep time: 15 minutes
Serves: 4

Ingredients:

1½ pounds beef steak (1-inch thick)
4 cloves garlic, minced and divided
3 tablespoons dried rosemary, crushed
Salt and black pepper, to taste
2 tablespoons coconut oil, divided
1 small onion, chopped
1 pound white mushrooms, sliced
1 pound asparagus, trimmed and cut into 2-inch pieces
1 tablespoon fresh lemon zest, grated

Instructions:

1. With a sharp knife, make deep cuts in steak.

2. In a bowl, mix together half of all garlic, rosemary, salt and black pepper.

3. Rub the garlic mixture on both sides of steak evenly.

4. In a skillet, heat 2 teaspoons oil on medium heat.

5. Add steak and cook for 5 minutes per side.

6. Transfer steak into a plate and cover with a foil paper to keep it warm.

7. In same skillet, heat remaining oil.

8. Add onion and sauté for 2 to 2½ minutes.

9. Add remaining garlic and sauté for 30 seconds.

10. Add mushrooms and asparagus and cook, stirring occasionally for about 5 minutes or till vegetables become tender and all liquid is absorbed.

11. Stir in remaining rosemary and lemon zest.

12. Season with salt and black pepper.

13. Cut steak in bite size pieces and place over a serving plate.

14. Serve with vegetables.

Nutritional Facts Per Serving:

Calories: 340
Fat: 14.9g
Carbohydrates: 13.1g
Protein: 41.0g

CHICKEN & PEAS SOUP

Cooking time: 1 hour
Prep time: 15 minutes
Serves: 4

Ingredients:

1 teaspoon coconut oil
2 cups boneless chicken, cut into bite-sized pieces
1 cup sweet onion, chopped
3 cloves garlic, minced
2 cups fresh peas, shelled
4 cups chicken broth
1 cup spinach, trimmed and wilted
Salt and black pepper, to taste

Instructions:

1. In a large pan, heat oil on medium heat.

2. Add chicken, onion and garlic and sauté for 4 to 5 minutes.

3. Add peas and broth and bring to a boil.

4. Reduce heat to medium-low.

5. Cover and simmer for 40 to 50 minutes.

6. Add spinach and season with salt and black pepper.

7. Cook for 4 to 5 minutes more.

Nutritional Facts Per Serving:

Calories: 257
Fat: 8.0g
Carbohydrates: 15.0g
Protein: 29.7g

Salmon Soup

Cooking time: 45 minutes
Prep time: 10 minutes
Serves: 4

Ingredients:

1 tablespoon coconut oil
1 cup onion, chopped
4 medium carrots, peeled and chopped
1 cup celery, chopped
3 cups vegetable broth
1 tablespoon paprika
1 teaspoon dried thyme
1½ pounds salmon fillet, cubed
Salt and black pepper, to taste

Instructions:

1. In a large pan, heat oil on medium heat.

2. Add onion, carrots and celery and sauté for 4 to 5 minutes.

3. Add broth, paprika and thyme and bring to a boil.

4. Reduce heat to low.

5. Simmer for 30 to 35 minutes.

6. Add salmon and season with salt and black pepper.

7. Cook for 10 minutes.

Nutritional Facts per Serving:

Calories: 456
Fat: 25.9g
Carbohydrates: 11.1g
Protein: 42.6g

CONCLUSION

CrossFit was founded and organized by Greg Glassman in the mid-1990s. He felt that current fitness programs were grossly lacking in key elements. As he worked with celebrities and professional athletes in Pasadena, California, he noticed that even the best of the best were not truly fit. Each had large gaps in their fitness abilities. Even worse, he noticed that many police, fire and military personnel were also in poor physical condition. This was not only unhealthy, it was deadly. As Glassman used to say "It is a lot harder to kill a fit person". Today, the key idea about CrossFit means that everyone can be fit. Everyone. This includes you. Start and you will succeed.

The purpose of CrossFit is to cover all 10 areas of fitness. These domains include cardiovascular and respiratory endurance, stamina, strength, flexibility, power, speed, coordination, balance, agility and accuracy. It is designed to be excruciating but also to be accomplished within a community. CrossFit is an exercise regimen that focuses on core and conditioning. It includes some common exercises like jump rope, along with other non-conventional ones like dragging a 300 pound log behind you. No matter where you fall on the fitness continuum, you are eligible to participate. Keep a journal of your training sessions and you will see how quickly you improve. CrossFit was designed for you.

The great thing about CrossFit is that it is nearly everywhere on earth. So if you travel a lot, or are taking a vacation, you can visit one of the 4000 CrossFit gyms all over the world. You can also meet other CrossFitters online and talk about your goals and concerns. CrossFit athletes love to talk about their fitness levels and to provide advice and support for others. If you have a family, then your kids too can participate in CrossFit Kids. CrossFit is a great activity to do for the whole family. You will build camaraderie and a love of fitness with your children.

CrossFit training involves lifting weights, resistance training and endurance. Free weights and barbells are used frequently in the WOD. CrossFit always has extremely high expectations and tend to push participants to their absolute physical limit. The key component is the WOD and if you do not belong to a CrossFit gym you can see many WOD videos on the CrossFit website. The videos are led by certified CrossFit trainers who show you how to make adaptations if needed. Remember that anyone can do CrossFit.

Other than the physical demands of CrossFit, the hardest part for many people will be to make changes to their diet. CrossFit recommends following the Paleo or Zone diets which are based on the equal distribution of protein, carbs, and fat. In short, the CrossFit attitude is, if the food is not perishable in a day or two, do not eat it! Stay away from processed foods and refined sugars. No matter how hard this may seem, after a week or two of changing your diet, you will feel so much better and you will never want to eat processed foods again.

As a final thought, remember that you can succeed at CrossFit. The fact that you are reading this demonstrates that you have already taken the first step in making the fitness commitment. You can be fit and you will be fit.

RESOURCES FOR FURTHER INFORMATION ABOUT CROSSFIT

WEBSITES
CrossFit Website | www.crossfit.com

This is a large website with many sub-sites. You will find information about gyms, classes, games, competitions and more. The CrossFit website is huge, so do not be intimidated. Take your time and use the search feature. From basic information to events for professional CrossFit athletes, you can find it all here.

CrossFit Facebook | www.facebook.com/crossfit

This is a great place to learn about things in a smaller venue than the huge official site. The amount of content is less, but you can get a feel for the online community and maybe see if any of the FB users are from your area.

CrossFit Journal | journal.crossfit.com

The CrossFit journal is updated weekly. There are archives of articles and pod casts, interviews with CrossFit trainers, and athletes and more. The articles here are the best anywhere. You can learn how to improve your technique, learn about nutrition and virtually anything there is to help you reach your fitness goals.

CrossFit YouTube Channel | youtube.com/user/CrossFitHQ/videos

This site is pay dirt for those of you who love videos!

ARTICLES

Jonathan Barba, "CrossFit PHYSICAL TRAINING," Law & Order, June 2005 | **www.questia.com/read/1P3-862693271**.

This article focuses on how police and fire departments have used CrossFit and how it has helped them.

Inside the Cult of CrosFit |

health.yahoo.net/articles/fitness/inside-cult-crossfit

This article explains what CrossFit is from one person's experience. If you are still unsure about how CrossFit will feel at first, this is the article to read. It is from an average young man's perspective.

We're One Big Team So Run Those Stairs.

http://www.nytimes.com/2013/03/31/business/crossfit-offers-an-exercise-in-corporate-teamwork-too.html

This article features a company in Colorado and how they used CrossFit to get fit in more ways than one. You will learn more about what it feels like to work in a community.

Inside the Box: How CrossFit; Shredded the Rules, Stripped Down the Gym, and Rebuilt My Body.By T.J Murphy.

www.amazon.com/dp/1934030902

This is the story of a well-trained athlete who had suffered a serious injury and was determined to get his fitness back. This is his story about how CrossFit was able to do this for him.

Training for The CrossFit Games: A Year of Programming Used to Train Julie Foucher, The 2nd Fittest Woman on Earth, CrossFit Games 2012
www.amazon.com/dp/B00C1NCNFY

Paleo Cookbook for Athletes – Lose Weight And Get Muscle Quickly And Easily With The Paleo Solution

www.amazon.com/dp/B00FJ30XUU

WHY ARE SO MANY PEOPLE FAILING? GET MY FREE REPORT

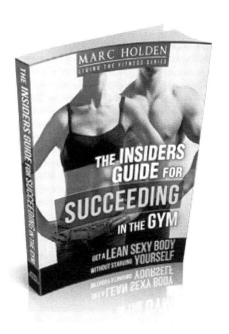

A lot of people seem to be failing after all the hard work in the gym. There is #1 reason why these people (and maybe you?) are failing and wasting their time in the gym right now.

In this free report I explain how you can succeed in your home gym. So grab your free copy of '**The Insiders Guide for Succeeding in the Gym**' now at livingthefitness.com/succeeding-gym/ and get that body you desire.

THANK YOU!

Thanks a lot for reading my book. I really hope you liked it and you learned a few things. If you have any questions you can mail me at **marc@livingthefitness.com**

If you liked this book or found it helpful, please leave me an honest review on Amazon. It's the best compliment I can get and it will help more people to find my book easily. Also any feedback is welcome so I can improve my books in the future.

Become a fan on Facebook for free great content. Join us today at **facebook.com/livingthefitness**

Or follow us at Twitter: **twitter.com/livingfitness1**

In this book we already discussed the importance of nutrition. Below you can read a chapter of my book about the Paleo diet.

Excerpt from *"Paleo for Athletes: Lose Weight and Get Muscle Quickly and Easily with the Paleo Solution"*

WHY THE PALEO DIET?

When starting any diet there should be two main questions you ask yourself, and they are:

- Why am I starting this diet?
- Can I live the life I need to with this diet?

If you cannot answer both of these questions in relation to any diet, then you need to get yourself something more suitable to your standards and style. So, what would the answers be if you were to start a Paleo diet?

To start off, the Paleo diet has been in circulation for about...two million years! About ten thousand years ago the human race changed its diet quite drastically when we started to eat things like grains and dairy. This is why so many people have intolerances to dairy, as our digestive system is not quite ready for it yet.

However, it has had a long, long time to get used to what you eat on a Paleo diet, which is the traditional stuff – fruits, vegetables, meats, nuts, and seeds. We have eaten this food for years and it has always been agreeable with our digestive systems, making it a no-brainer.

We have been eating the foods in a Paleo diet since day one, but with more modern foods like dairy, we have been consuming them for roughly 0.4% of our existence. Since we have moved into this new period of eating the foods we consume today, humanity has suffered quite a bit more with regards to health issues.

We have replaced the foods we use to eat with a series of low nutrition and high toxic meals that just damage our system, and do not provide it with what we need to live. Humanity has become smaller, we have more bone troubles these days, illnesses like cancer have become more common, diabetes is rife in certain countries, and things like skin problems and heart disease are on the rise constantly.

This is to do with our diets – before we changed to our current diets, we ate what made us healthy and made us strong. Today, we eat sugary goods that ruin our bodies over time and do untold damage.

A Paleo diet takes you back to your roots – it puts you back on a healthy lifestyle and removes all of the nonsense that we aren't ready to eat. Maybe in another 50,000 years our digestive system will be ready to cope with all of this junk, but today it is simply not prepared.

A Paleo diet cuts out all of the toxins we put into our systems and replaces them with natural supplements and nutrients, giving you a much healthier body as a result. Not only that, you are still given a huge amounts of foods to choose from when it comes to eating! So this is a fun diet to be on where you can mix it up and still enjoy your foods, all the while receiving the benefits you get from eating much cleaner!

End of excerpt from *"Paleo for Athletes: Lose Weight and Get Muscle Quickly and Easily with the Paleo Solution"*

If you are interested in reading more about the Paleo diet. Grab your copy today at **Amazon.com** and start eating to get lean!

Take care,

Marc

Made in the USA
San Bernardino, CA
03 January 2014